DESIGNS & PATTERNS FROM
NORTH AFRICAN
CARPETS & TEXTILES

DESIGNS & PATTERNS FROM
NORTH AFRICAN
CARPETS & TEXTILES

JACQUES REVAULT
Head, Tunisian Arts Department, Tunisian Ministry of National Economy

DOVER PUBLICATIONS, INC., NEW YORK

Published in Canada by General Publishing Company, Ltd., 30 Lesmill Road, Don Mills, Toronto, Ontario.
Published in the United Kingdom by Constable and Company, Ltd., 10 Orange Street, London WC 2.

This Dover edition, first published in 1973, is a new selection, by Jacques Revault, of plates from the four portfolios of *Tapis tunisiens*, by L. Poinssot and J. Revault, originally published by Horizons de France, Paris, as follows: I, *"Kairouan" et imitations*, 2nd revised and enlarged edition, 1955; II, *Tapis bédouins à haute laine*, 1950; III, *Tissus décorés de Gafsa et imitations*, 1953; and IV, *Tissus ras décorés de Kairouan, du Sâḥel et du Sud tunisien*, 1957. A new brief text has been written by Mr. Revault specially for the present edition, and has been translated by Stanley Appelbaum. This edition is published by special arrangement with Horizons de France.

International Standard Book Number: 0-486-22850-9
Library of Congress Catalog Card Number: 72-93604

Manufactured in the United States of America
Dover Publications, Inc.
180 Varick Street
New York, N.Y. 10014

CONTENTS

TUNISIAN CARPETS

Carpet weaving in Tunisia, where it has long been practiced, presents the same diversity as in the other parts of the Maghreb, Algeria and Morocco.

Here too we find a distinction between city-made carpets with Eastern-inspired floral ornamentation and rural carpets with geometric (or strongly stylized) decoration that is archaic in appearance.

The two principal techniques known throughout North Africa are also employed here: knotting (velvety pile fastened between warp and weft) and flat weaving (taffeta weave on warp and weft).

With the exception of a very few Bedouin carpets made by professional weavers, the manufacture of carpets on high-warp looms is essentially women's work. Just like esparto mats and woolen blankets and garments, carpets are also produced in the midst of the family. One among many household chores, carpet making is a traditional occupation which a good number of Tunisian women practice at home.

CITY-MADE KNOTTED-PILE CARPETS:
THE "KAIROUAN" AND IMITATIONS
(Plates 1-30)

Compared with the carpets of Rabat in Morocco and Setif in Algeria, with which it shares similar influences, the Kairouan carpet (*zerbîya*) gives the appearance of an imitation of Anatolian carpets.

It is said to have been introduced to the Holy City by the daughter of a Turkish governor in the mid-nineteenth century.

The first carpets produced in this fashion remained a luxury reserved for the wealthiest households in Kairouan. Some of them were also presented by donors to mosques and religious schools.

They reflect the original composition of the Ghiordes carpets with their hexagonal field surrounded by spandrels and border stripes. Ornamental motifs, most frequently floral, occur in repeat in a color harmony with red, blue and green dominants. In the past these colors were obtained from natural sources (cochineal, madder, indigo, woad, weld, etc.). But in order to meet local needs it became necessary to adapt the imitations of Eastern models to the proportions of Kairouan apartments; hence their characteristic length. Small dimensions were retained only for prayer carpets and saddle rugs.

When Tunisia became a French protectorate, carpet weaving became general in the city; the townswomen were already familiar with the operations of carding and spinning wool, as well as the manufacture of clothing and blankets.

Esteemed by a new European clientele, the "Kairouan" became a major household industry of world repute. It gave rise to a variation on the original theme, without vivid colors, the "alloucha" (*ᶜallûša*).

vii

In most families the technique of knotting and the knowledge of the traditional motifs are handed down from mother to daughter. These motifs thus form a repertoire familiar to the weavers, who identify and name them after common objects they resemble: bouquet (*mešmûm*), bird (*ʿaṣfûr*), rose (*werd*), vase (*fânûz*), assembly (*ḥaḍra*), moon (*qamra*), lion's paw (*keff eṣ-ṣîd*), bride wearing a belt (*ʿarûṣa mḥezzma*), snake and frog (*ḥneš û jrân*), pomegranate (*rommân*), etc.

The fashion of the "Kairouan" has spread in the cities and has in its turn resulted in more or less faithful imitations from north to south in Tunisia, particularly in Bizerte and Gabès. This carpet is in especially great demand for wedding celebrations, where it represents one of the essential elements of the furnishings.

BEDOUIN THICK-PILE KNOTTED CARPETS
(Figures A-D; Plates 31-59)

The thick-pile Bedouin carpets woven in Tunisia resemble the *qṭîf* or *qṭîfa* of Algeria (Constantine region and Djebel Amour) and Morocco (Atlas region). Their production—almost at a standstill today—was especially famous in the past among the tribes of central and southern Tunisia (Hamâma, Zlass, Maḥadba) and a few northern tribes (Drîd, Ouled Bou Ghanem).

The Bedouin carpet, like the "Kairouan," originated in the East, but earlier. It is said that the models of the *qṭîf* were brought back by travelers and merchants, and by pilgrims returning from Mecca. But the coarser weave of Tunisian carpets inevitably made their appearance quite different from that of the carpets which had inspired them.

As opposed to the Kairouan carpets, the production of Bedouin carpets was seasonal. They were very expensive and were only made on order for tribal chieftains or wealthy oasis proprietors. Manufacture was begun in summer or autumn after sheep-shearing and the end of harvest. Then a nomad weaver (*reggâm*) noted for his skill would be called in. Festivities were organized in his honor at the beginning and at the end of his work. With the aid of two women, he had to compose and direct the manufacture of a *qṭîfa* (Figure A shows the elements of a Bedouin loom). The motifs which he carried in his head were most often geometric. Sometimes they had a magic meaning that helped to increase the importance of the carpet. When the carpet was finished and removed from the vertical loom, it was spread out on the ground to be admired by everyone. It was thus possible to observe that the two sides were very different, one with a flat surface showing rectangular subdivisions, or a succession of compartments, filled with geometric motifs conceived by the *reggâm* (see Figures B–D), the other presenting a thick fleece with warm polychromy dominated by red and blue.

The decorative elements represented were either rounded objects depicted in a schematic cruciform fashion—moon (*gamra*), circle (*dûra*), ball (*karkûba*), seal or ring (*ḥâtem*), "Eastern horn" (*garn šergi*)—or familiar objects repeated in the form of checkers or diamonds—arches (*ʿaqwâs*), window grille (*šabbâk*), saw (*mûnšar*), a game similar to checkers (*ḥarbga*), palms (*jrâîd*).

The *qṭîfa* was ordinarily used as mattress and blanket for a whole family during the cold winter nights. When not used in this way, this carpet remained a luxury object unrolled only on the occasion of certain family feasts (weddings, circumcisions) or to celebrate the visit of a distinguished guest.

Fig. A: A typical Bedouin loom. 1: Beams. 2: Uprights. 3: Cords attaching the upper beam to the uprights. 4: Straining nails. 5: Stretchers. 6: Shed stick. 7 and 8: Reeds in the warp.

Fig. B: Bedouin carpet design with a rectangular field divided into three sections.

Fig. C: Bedouin carpet design with a rectangular field divided into four sections separated by strong borders.

Fig. D: Bedouin carpet design with a series of compartments running lengthwise.

DECORATED TEXTILES FROM GAFSA AND IMITATIONS
(Plates 60-86)

Gafsa (the ancient Capsa), a south Tunisian oasis located at the crossroads of the main north-south and east-west caravan routes, is justly famous for the originality of its decorated wool blankets.

The home weaving industry has been known there for several centuries. But it has not been possible to trace the origin of the special ornamentation that distinguishes the Gafsa blankets, *fraš* (or *ḥûli*) and *ferrâštya* (or *baṭṭanîya*), from the other decorated textiles that are so widespread throughout Tunisia. We can merely note their resemblance to the carpets of Haouz and the Haut-Atlas in Morocco and certain textiles of Greece, Anatolia and Persia. The ornamentation of Gafsa blankets, distributed in compartments and rectangles, is composed not only of geometric motifs but also of animate subjects; the rectilinear decorative elements are based on squares, triangles and diamonds with cusped notches, frequently repeated according to custom. The women who weave these blankets derive the inspiration for this schematized expression—in this case there is no "right" or "wrong" side of the cloth—from their household interiors and from the oasis familiar to them. That is why they are equally tempted to depict the arches of their modest porticos (*ᶜaqwâs*), a nomad tent (*bît*), a tortoise (*fakrûn*), a snake (*ḥneš*), a line of fish they might have seen in an irrigation canal (*ḥût*), a camel caravan (*jmel*), the soldiers of the nearby fortified palace standing at attention (*ᶜasker*) or merchants aligned in their booths. Sometimes they risk conjuring up more impressive figures, such as General Forgemol —who entered Gafsa in 1881—or a roaring lion. The stiff and angular human silhouettes are always shown frontally, the animals in profile—the lion, however, retaining its head full-width.

This archaic ornament is sustained by a sober coloration of red, blue, green, yellow and black on a white background. It completely covers the square blankets (*ferrâštya*), but is confined to the ends of the *fraš* blankets, which are from 16 to 32 feet long.

Much sought after by the citizens of Tunis (Moslems and Jews) and the other chief cities of Tunisia, the *fraš* has long been a major article of trade with the other parts of the Maghreb (Algeria and Tripolitania).

The success of the decorated textiles of Gafsa can only be compared to that of the Kairouan carpet. Thus they have given rise to just as many imitations, sometimes resulting in curious interpretations, extending from the region of Gabès to the region of Testour and even beyond the Algerian border (Nememcha and Haracta).

DECORATED FLAT-WOVEN TEXTILES OF KAIROUAN, THE SÂḤEL AND SOUTHERN TUNISIA
(Plates 87-121)

Because of Tunisia's temperate climate, the household industry of flat weaving is much more predominant than that of knotted-pile carpets. The same rudimentary high-warp loom has led to the production of black or striped cloths for garments and to the manufacture of carpets and decorated blankets.

Of recent origin, these last-named textiles have spread widely from north to south in the eastern Maghreb, some manufactured in the houses of cities or market towns, others in the tents of encampments.

DECORATED TEXTILES OF KAIROUAN
(Plates 87-101)

Coming after the traditional textiles adorned with simple stripes, the decorated textiles of the Holy City made their appearance in the wealthy home of a kaid of Kairouan, thanks to the presence of women from the south of Tunisia and Tripolitania who were expert in the ornamentation of cloths for garments (*baḥnûq*).

Just like the first *zerbîya*, the new decorated *klim* and *mergûm* remained at the start the prerogative of a few rich families before they became in their turn the products of a commercialized industry.

They actually represented a more complex art than that of the knotted carpet or the Gafsa blanket with reversible decoration. In fact, here the weaver had to learn to work "blind" on the reverse of the cloth, faced with a warp of intermingled colored threads. This forced her to use mnemonic rhymes in order to envision the motifs she wished to execute, which would be visible only on the "right" side of the cloth. This innovation made it possible to make the same products—though different in appearance—as with knotting: saddle rugs (*bešṭ*), prayer carpets (*klim*) and rugs that were partly striped and partly ornamented (*klim-mergûm*) or entirely ornamented (*mergûm*). To these products was added a wall hanging (*haïṭi*) for the bed alcove or the reception room.

Sometimes alternating with stripes, the designs are exclusively geometric, made up chiefly of sawtooth elements, triangles and diamonds with various designations: a sultan's banner (*ʿalîm Sulṭân*), bride (*ʿarûṣa*), amulet (*ḥrûz*), apple (*teffâḥ*), ewer (*brîq*), couscous container (*keskâs*), rings (*ḫwâtem*), tortoise (*fukrûn*), etc. The composition of these elements did not fail to change and evolve, retaining the transverse arrangement of the traditional *klim*, adopting the distribution in longitudinal compartments of the Bedouin *ḥamel*, or imitating the field and borders of the *zerbîya*.

The first Kairouan weavers also copied this carpet's gentle color harmony, based on red and almond green heightened with black, white, blue and pale yellow.

Later this felicitous polychromy disappeared and was replaced by the neutral shades of the modern *zerbîya* called "alloucha."

DECORATED TEXTILES OF THE SÂHEL
(Plates 102-115)

The beauty of the Sâḥel textiles is justly famous in the villages of El-Djem, La Chebba, Bou-Merdâs and Djebeniana. It is indeed evident in the ornamental richness of their women's shawls (*mendîl, mûšṭîya*), their cushions (*ûsâda*), blankets (*klim, wazra*) and hangings (*ksâya*). The geometric repertoire and the technique of the decorated textiles, related to those of Kairouan, are said to have come from Tripolitania. These cloths represent a great diversity of multicolored motifs set off with white cotton. The weavers identify these motifs as follows: zigzag (*ʿarrûj*), bride (*ʿarûṣa*), gardens (*bestân*), beans (*fûl*), bracelet (*ḥdîda*), snake (*ḥneš*), fish (*ḥût*), palm tree (*nḫal*), tattooing (*ušâm*), etc.

More care is always expended on pieces for family use than on those intended for market sale. The former category includes the *ûsâda, klim, ksâya* and *wazra*, which every man must bring to his new home at marriage.

As elsewhere, the manufacture of these textiles is accompanied by invocations to God and the Prophet, amulets and fumigations to drive away spirits, not to mention visits to local holy men.

DECORATED TEXTILES OF OUDREF
(Plates 116-121)

The oasis of Oudref, near Gabès, is no less reputed than the places just mentioned for the quality and originality of its decorated wool textiles. In each brown-earth dwelling, one or more looms are to be found in a room, courtyard portico or entrance corridor.

The women work at them without let-up in all seasons, carding, spinning, weaving, from sunrise to sunset. Some of them are making blankets which they prepare in advance for their sons' weddings, blankets soberly adorned with stripes and infrequent brown motifs on white (*baṭṭâna* and *ferrâša*), which accompany the *ḥambel*, the principal, large-scale blanket adorned with stripes of indigo blue, madder red and a black derived from pomegranate peels, heightened with three similar white cotton bands containing geometric ornament: scorpion (*ᶜagreb*), snail (*babûša*), horn (*gern*), knife (*sekkîn*), etc. The fiancée, for her part, will complete the bedding by contributing a cushion (*ûsâda*) that she has decorated in the same way.

Elsewhere textiles intended for market sale are manufactured: saddle rugs (*bešṭ*) that are in great demand among the tribal horsemen, blankets imitated from the *ḥambel* (*mergûm nwîrî*)—which are themselves copied in other southern localities (El-Ḥamma, Maṭmâṭa, etc.)—flat-woven carpets entirely or partially decorated with polychrome designs trimmed with white on a red background. These last-mentioned textiles constitute a new industry which supplies rugs, prayer carpets and wall hangings.

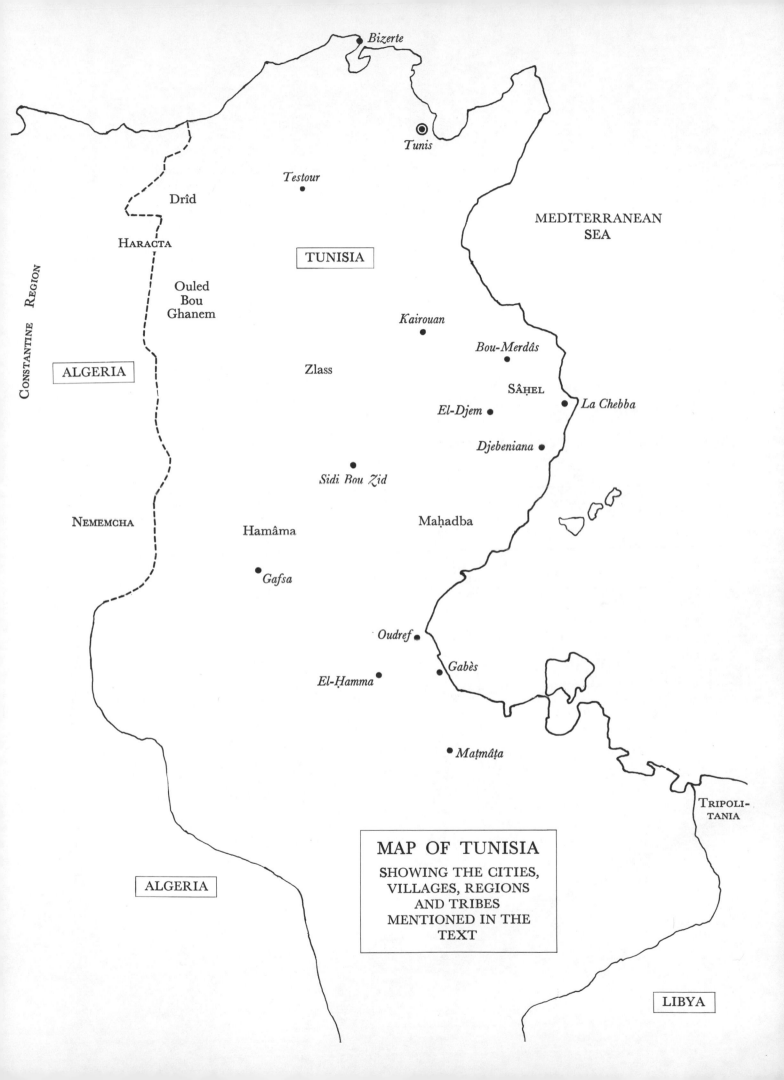

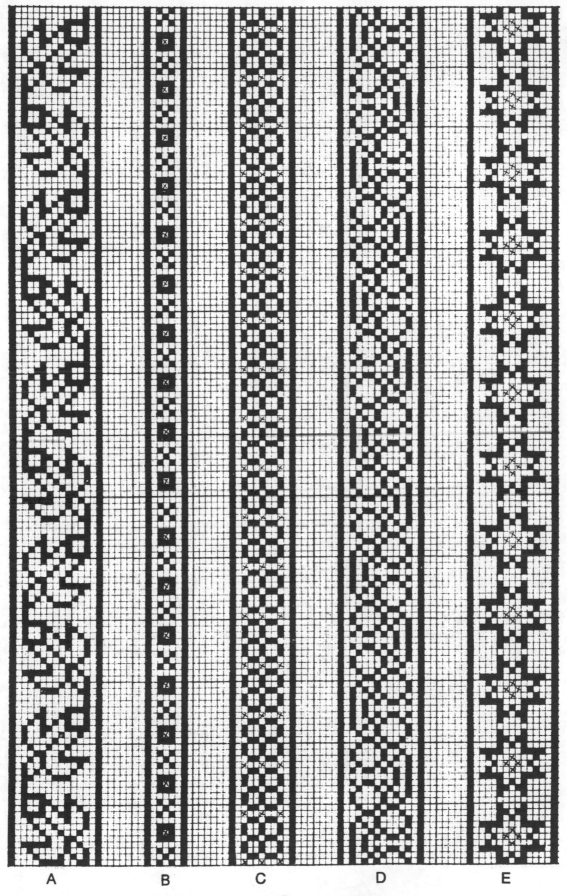

1 "Kairouan" carpet (*zerbíya*) motifs. A: Sparrows. B: Squares of dough. C: Roses. D: Grapes. E: Stars.

A   B   C   D   E

2 "Kairouan" carpet motifs. A: "His hand in his
brother's hand." B: Earrings. C: Red peppers. D: Roses
in small boats. E: Watches.

A   B   C   D

3 "Kairouan" carpet motifs. A: Roses in boats. B:
Cakes. C: Plumed hats. D: Swallows.

4 "Kairouan" carpet motifs. A: Turks. B: The
Lord's tiles. C: Boxes.

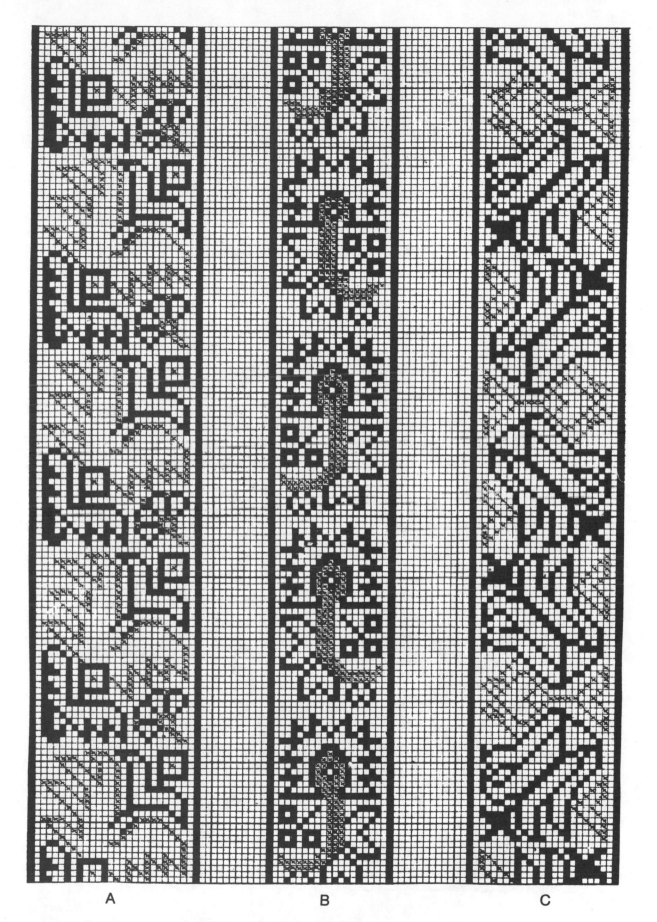

A   B   C

5 "Kairouan" carpet motifs. A: Lion's paws. B:
Crowns. C: Paws.

A   B

6   "Kairouan" carpet motifs. A: Bouquets. B: Trains,
or steamboats.

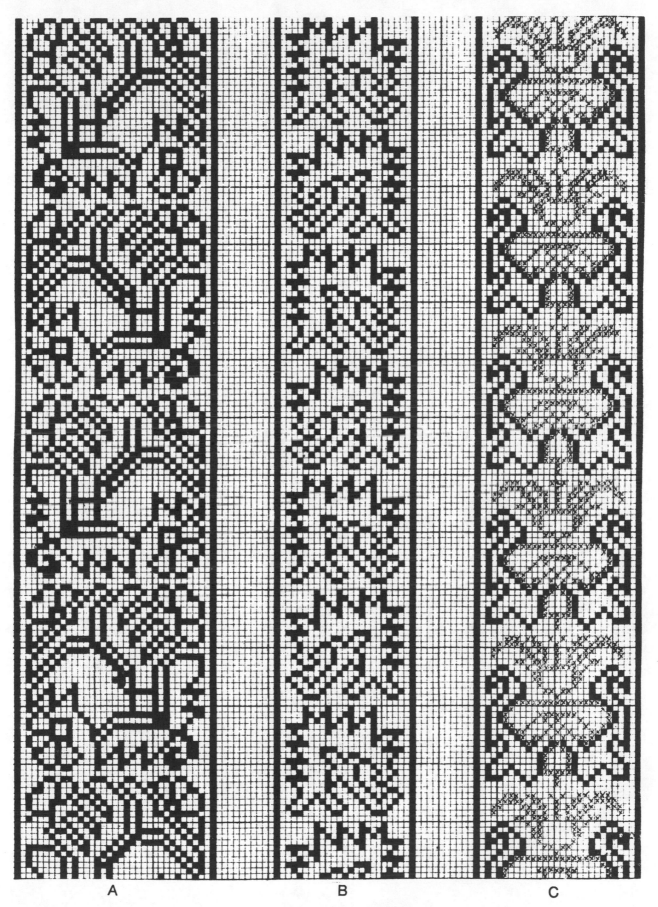

A   B   C

7 "Kairouan" carpet motifs. A: Lion's paws. B:
Bouquets. C: Brides wearing belts.

8 "Kairouan" carpet motifs. A: Arches. B: Snakes and frogs. C: Bouquets.

A   B

9   "Kairouan" carpet motifs. A: Pomegranates on branches. B: Bouquets.

A   B

10 "Kairouan" carpet motifs. A: Bouquets. B: Crowns.

11   "Kairouan" carpet motif: "The disorderly man at
the assembly."

12 "Kairouan" carpet motif: Animals.

13   "Kairouan" carpet motif: Bouquets.

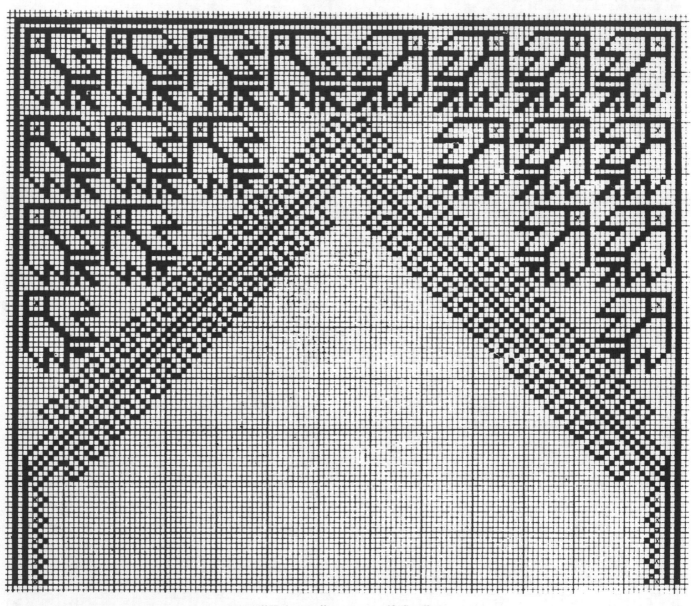

14 "Kairouan" carpet motif: Swallows.

15 "Kairouan" carpet motifs. A: Eight-branched
medallion. B: Four-branched medallion. C: Plumed
medallion. D: Hooked medallion.

16 "Kairouan" carpet motifs. A–C: Paws. D, E: Fish. F: Bird. G, H, L: "Ornaments." I, N, P, V: Roses. J, K: Ewers. M: Star. O: "The disorderly man at the assembly." Q, X: Bouquets. R: Petroleum lamp. S: Vase. T: Reel. U: Frog. W: Slipper.

17   "Kairouan" carpet motif: Assembly.

18 "Kairouan" carpet motif: Assembly with candles.

19 "Kairouan" pattern. From an antique *rekkâbíya* (saddle rug) in the Office des Arts Tunisiens, Centre de Kairouan, 29½″ × 27½″. The background of the field and the two guard stripes is cochineal red; of the inner border, white; of the outer border, light green.

20 "Kairouan" pattern. From an antique *zerbîya mtaᶜ ṣlâ* (prayer carpet) in the Office des Arts Tunisiens, Dar ᶜOthman, 55¼″ × 39⅜″. The background of the hexag-onal field is cochineal red; of the spandrels and the outer border, green; of the inner border, white; of the central border, red.

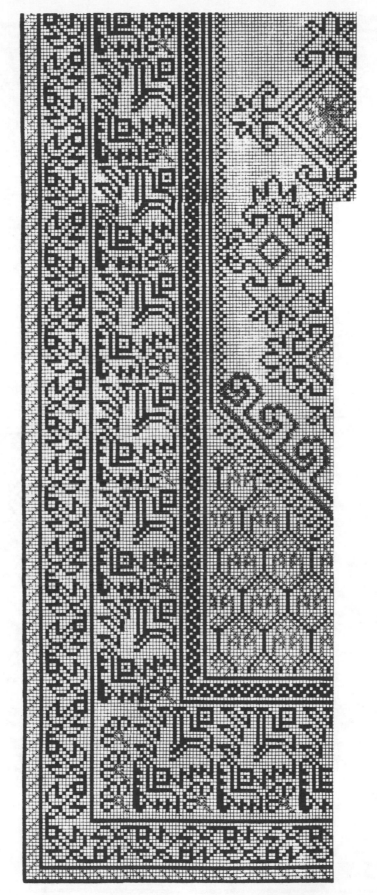

21 "Kairouan" pattern. From an antique carpet (*zerbíya*) in the Office des Arts Tunisiens, Dar ʿOthman, 61″ × 39⅞″. The background of the field is cochineal red; of the spandrels and the inner guard stripe, green; of the main border, blue; of the next adjoining guard stripe, red; of the outer one, blue and red.

22 "Kairouan" pattern. From an antique carpet,
90½" × 47¼". The background of the field is cochineal
red; of the spandrels and the outer border, blue; of the
inner border, white; of the central one, red.

23 "Kairouan" pattern. From an antique carpet, 98½″ × 48″. The background of the field is cochineal red; of the spandrels and the main border, blue-green; of the inner guard stripe, white; of the outer guard stripe, red.

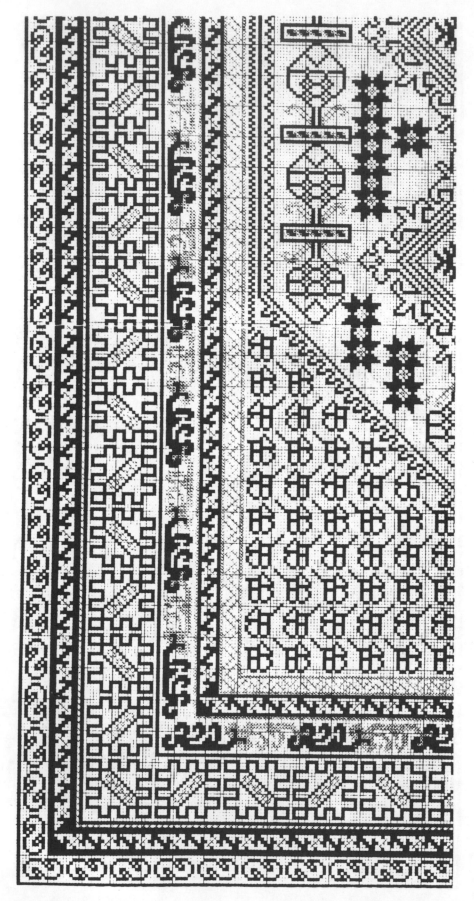

24 "Kairouan" pattern. From an antique carpet, $110\frac{1}{4}'' \times 55\frac{1}{8}''$. The background of the field is cochineal red; of the spandrels and the innermost guard stripe, blue-green; of the next adjoining guard stripe and the one next to the outermost one, black; of the third one from the center, white; of the main border, blue; of the outermost guard stripe, yellow.

25 "Kairouan" pattern. From an antique carpet, 106⅜″ × 55¼″. The background of the field is cochineal red; of the spandrels, the innermost guard stripe and the next-to-outermost guard stripe, blue-green; of the main border, blue; of the second guard stripe from the center and the outermost one, pink.

26 "Kairouan" pattern. From a reconstruction of an antique carpet in the Office des Arts Tunisiens, Dar Ben ʿAbd Allah, 206¾″ × 80¾″. The background of the field and the outermost guard stripe is red; of the spandrels, almond green; of the innermost guard stripe, white; of the main border, green; of the next guard stripe, pink.

27 "Kairouan" pattern. From an antique carpet, 187″ × 90½″. The background of the field is cochineal red; of the spandrels and the outer border, blue-green; of the innermost guard stripe and the third one from the center, pink; of the inner border, blue; of the second guard stripe from the center, white; of the next-to-outermost guard stripe, pink and blue; of the outermost one, red.

28 "Kairouan" patterns. All from one antique carpet,
116⅛″ × 65″. Colors predominantly cochineal red,
white and blue.

29 "Kairouan" pattern. From an antique carpet in the Musée du Bardo, Tunis, 207⅛" × 94⅝". The background of the field is cochineal red; of the spandrels, green; of the two guard stripes, white; of the inner and outer borders, red; of the central border, blue.

30 "Bizerte" pattern. From a modern local Bizerte imitation of "Kairouan" carpets, $153\frac{1}{2}'' \times 58\frac{7}{8}''$. The background of the field and the inner border is red; of the next border and the outermost one, white; of the next-to-outermost one, black. The designs in the field are sky blue, pink, violet, yellow, green, etc.

A   B   C   D

31   Bedouin carpet motifs (Hamâma tribe). A: Arches.
B: Chains. C, D: Jerboas.

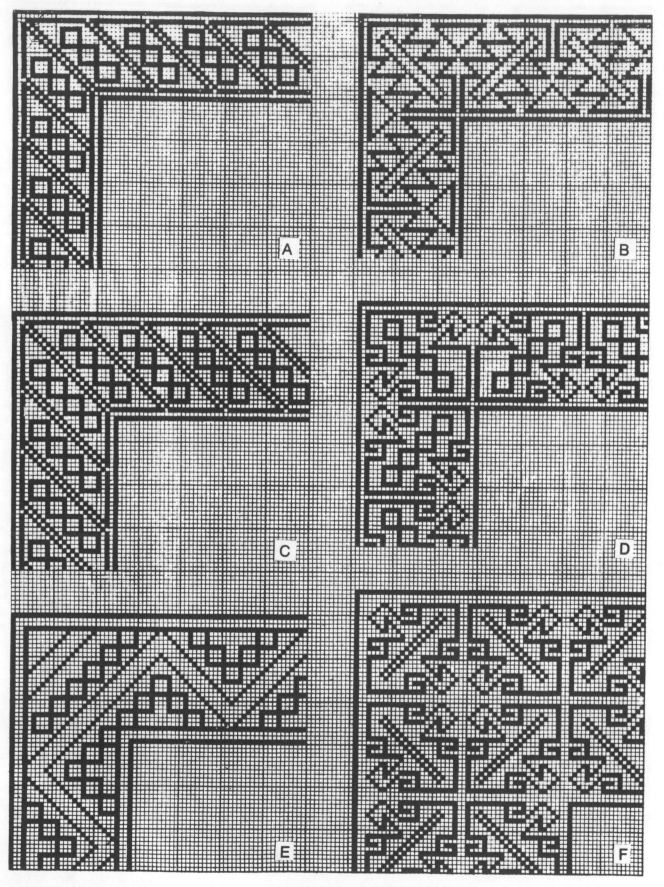

32 Bedouin carpet motifs (Hamâma tribe). A, C, D, E:
Palms. B: Saws. F: Wood carved in openwork.

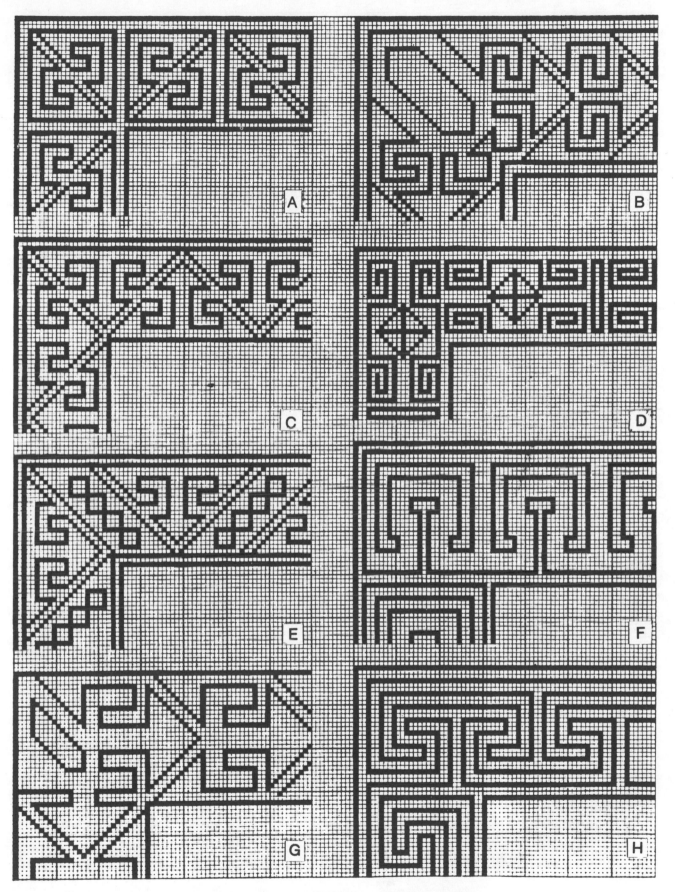

33 Bedouin carpet motifs (Hamâma tribe). A, B: "His hand in his brother's hand"; hooks. C: Hooks. D, F, H: Rings. E: Hooks and palms. G: Bottles.

A   B

34   Bedouin carpet motifs (Hamâma tribe): Two types
of "dizziness."

A   B   C

35 Bedouin carpet motifs (Hamâma tribe): Three
types of lion's paws.

36 Bedouin carpet motifs (Hamâma tribe). A, B, D:
Rings. C: "Dizziness"; rings.

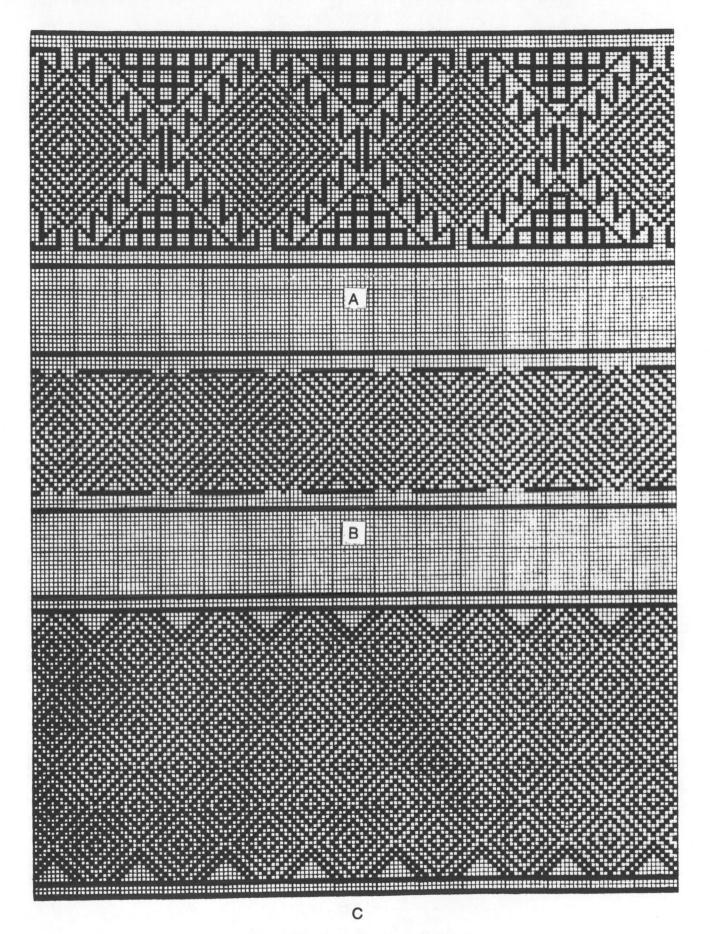

37 Bedouin carpet motifs (Hamâma tribe). A: Saws.
B, C: Jerboas.

A

B

38   Bedouin carpet motifs (Hamâma tribe): Two types
of arches.

A

B

39 Bedouin carpet motifs (Hamâma tribe): *Gettar* and "green" motifs.

40 Bedouin carpet motifs (Hamâma tribe). A, C, E:
"Eastern horns." B: Crenellations. D, F: Game boards.

41   Bedouin carpet motifs (Hamâma tribe). A, C, E:
Balls. B, D, F: Crenellations.

42 Bedouin carpet motifs (Hamâma tribe). A: Camel
with palanquin. B, E, H: Camels. C: Little animal.
D: Seven worthies. F: Pedestrian. G: Horseman.

43 Bedouin carpet motifs (Hamâma tribe): Three
types of rings.

44 Bedouin carpet motifs (Hamâma tribe). A: Ball.
B: Ring with cotton; "Eastern horn." C: Ring.

45   Bedouin carpet motifs (Hamâma tribe): Two types
of "moon with its sides."

46 Bedouin carpet motif (Hamâma tribe): "Eastern
horn."

47   Bedouin carpet motif (Hamâma tribe): "Eastern horn."

48 Bedouin carpet motif (Hamâma tribe): "Eastern horn."

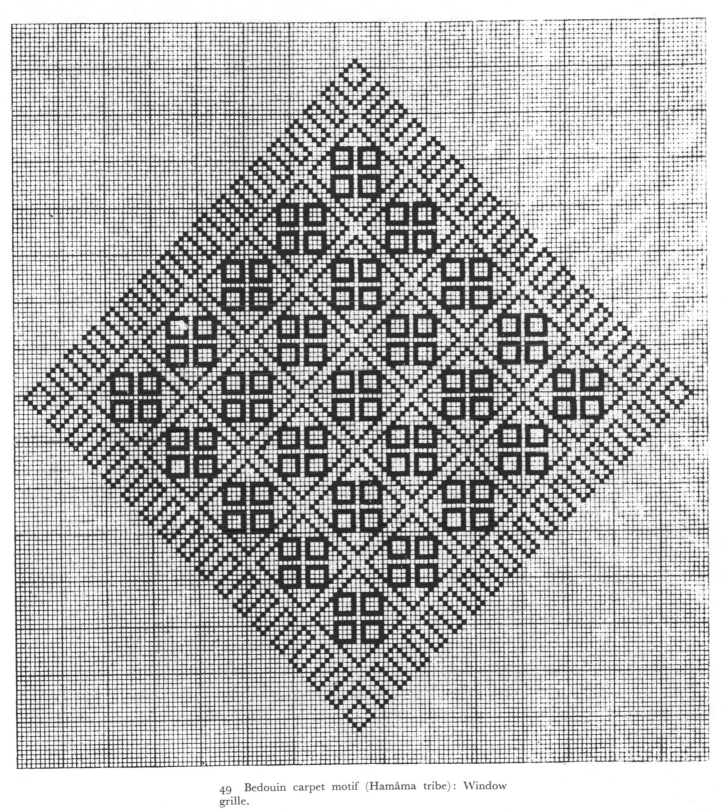

49 Bedouin carpet motif (Hamâma tribe): Window grille.

50 Bedouin carpet motif (Hamâma tribe): Window grille.

51 Bedouin carpet motif (Hamâma tribe).

52   Bedouin carpet motif (Hamâma tribe): "Eastern
horn."

53 Bedouin carpet motif (Hamâma tribe): "Moon with its sides."

54   Bedouin carpet motif (Hamâma tribe).

55   Bedouin carpet pattern (Hamâma tribe). From a
late nineteenth-century carpet in the Musée du Bardo,
Tunis, $146\frac{3}{4}'' \times 78\frac{3}{4}''$. Red background with designs in
blue, green, orange and white.

56 Bedouin carpet pattern (Hamâma tribe). From an antique carpet in the Office des Arts Tunisiens, 150¾" × 74¾". Violet background with designs in black, blue, green, mauve and white.

57 Bedouin carpet pattern (Hamâma tribe). From a
late nineteenth-century carpet in the Office des Arts
Tunisiens, $127\frac{7}{8}'' \times 70\frac{3}{4}''$. Red background with designs
in brown, blue, green, orange and white.

58 Bedouin carpet pattern (Hamâma tribe). From a
late nineteenth-century carpet in the Office des Arts
Tunisiens, 116⅛″ × 70¾″. Garnet background with
designs in dark blue, orange, green and white.

59 Bedouin carpet pattern (Hamâma tribe). From the
reverse side of a modern carpet in the Office des Arts
Tunisiens, 169¼″ × 82¼″. Red background with designs
in blue, black, orange, green and white.

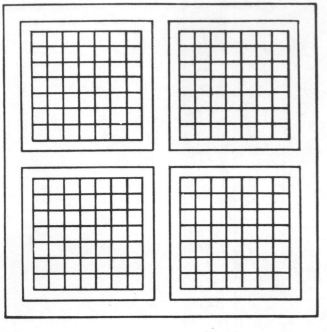

A

B

C

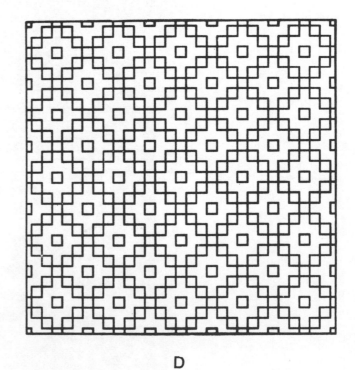

D

60 Gafsa textile motifs. A: Windows. B: Dominos. C:
Vases. D: Carvings.

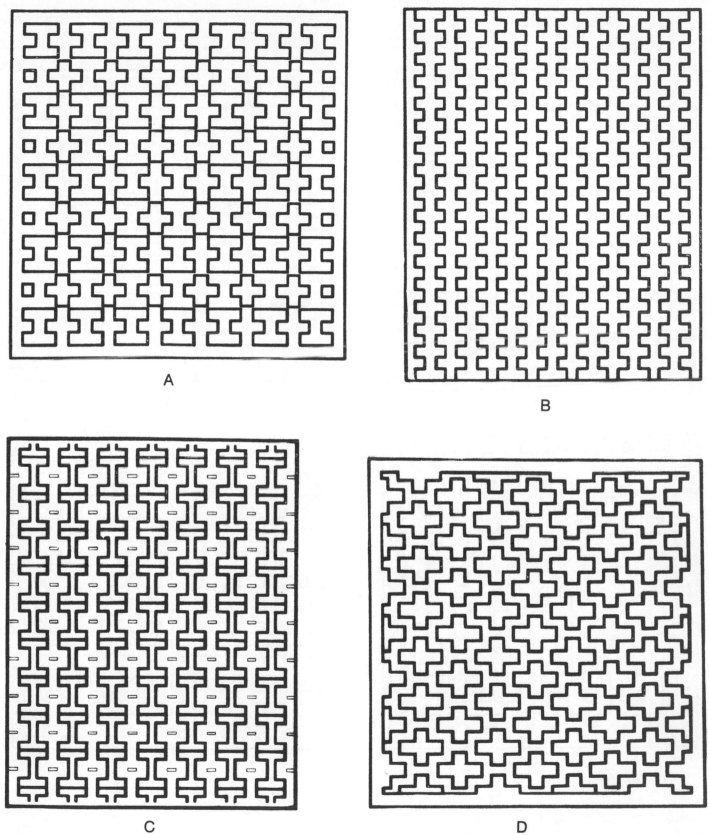

A

B

C

D

61   Gafsa textile motifs. A, D: Units. B, C: Combs.

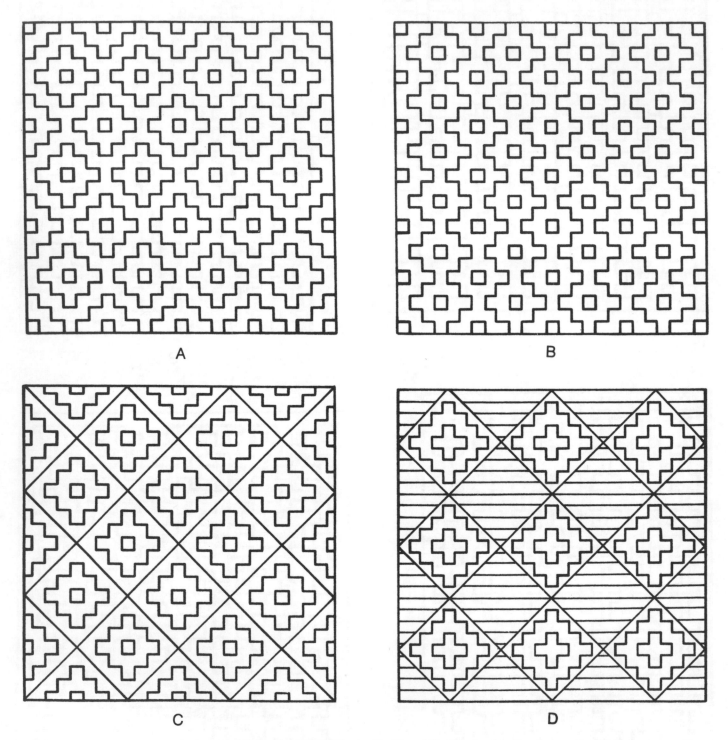

62 Gafsa textile motifs. A, C: Vases. B: Foreigners'
tombs. D: Pendentives.

63 . Gafsa textile motifs. A: Spider's webs. B: Webs with tents. C: Superimposed webs. D: Intermingled webs.

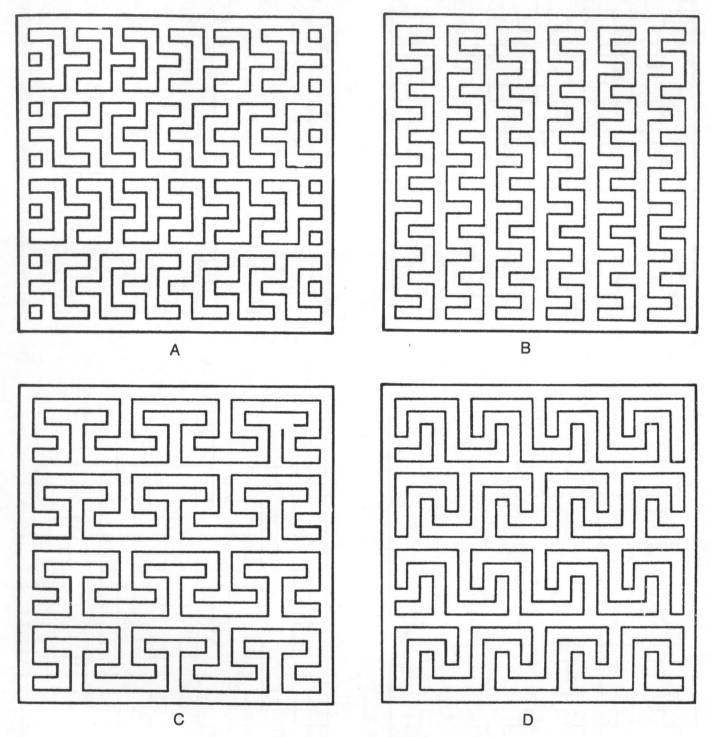

64 Gafsa textile motifs. A: Stretcher-grips; spurs. B:
Writing. C: Writing; keys. D: Threading.

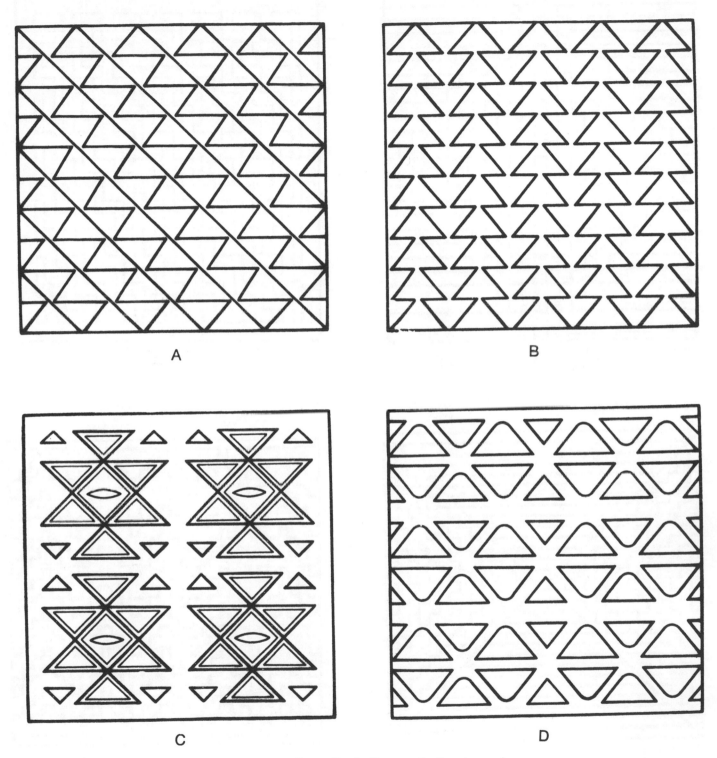

65 Gafsa textile motifs. A: Etagere. B: Leaning and raised. C: Birds. D: Flowers.

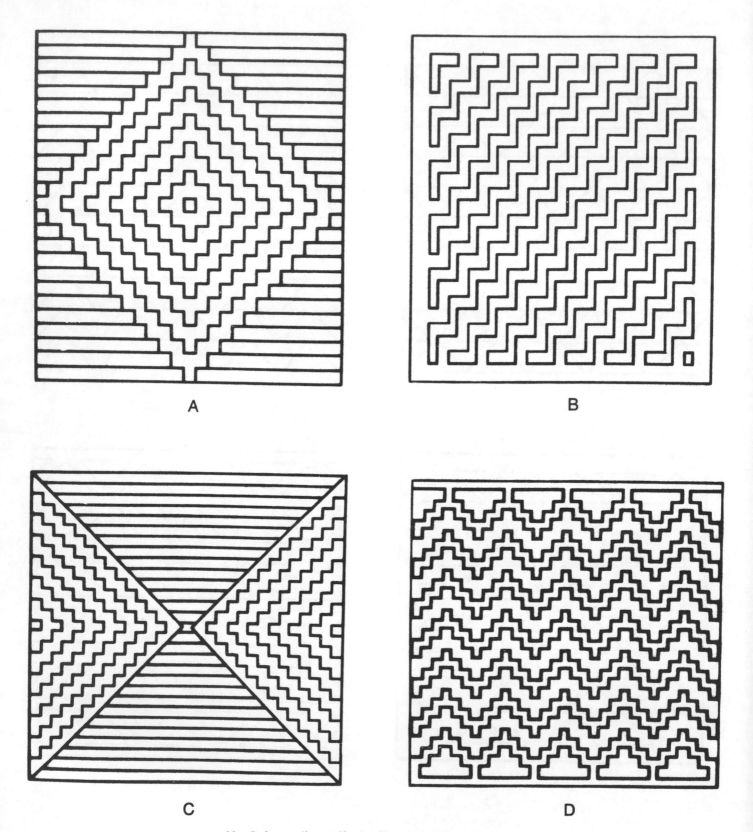

66 Gafsa textile motifs. A: Chamber with cheeks and spoons. B: Snakes. C: Chamber with heaps and spoons. D: Tebessa shawl.

67   Gafsa textile motifs. A: Chamber with heaps. B:
Tree-chamber; chamber with cheeks. C: Tortoises. D:
Chamber with lemons.

A

B

68 Gafsa textile motifs: Two types of chamber with
jasmine.

A

B

69   Gafsa textile motifs. A: Chamber with drinking
glasses. B: Chamber with porticos.

70 Gafsa textile motifs. A: Soldier's chamber. B:
Camel's chamber. C: Chamber with porticos. D:
Chained soldier.

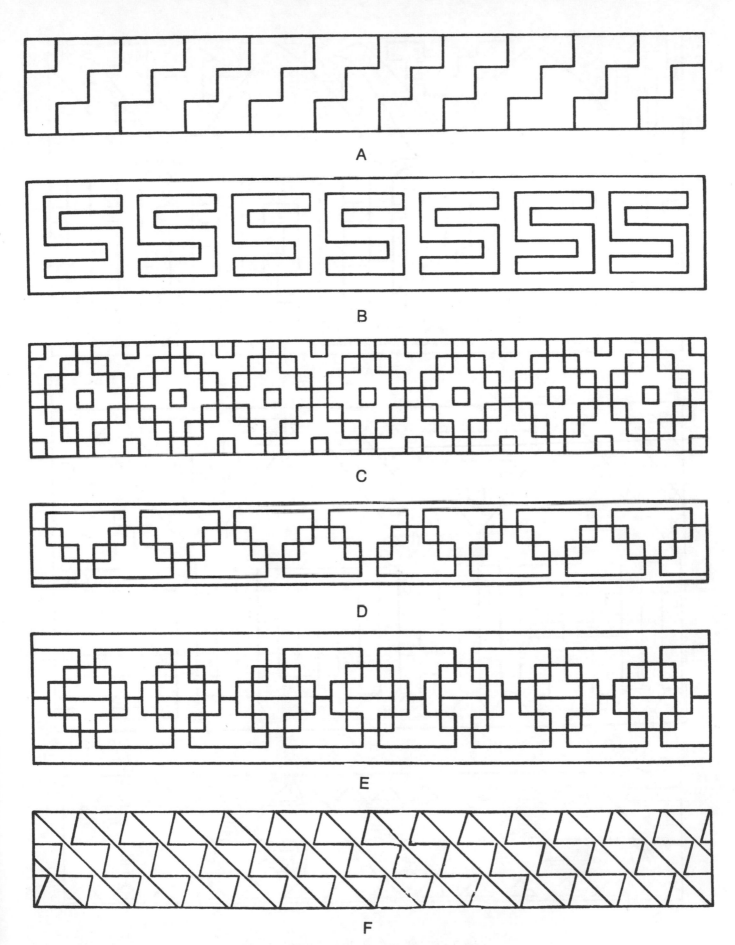

A

B

C

D

E

F

71 Gafsa textile motifs. A: Black and sky blue. B:
Writing. C: Carving. D: Spider's webs. E: Webs with
units. F: Etagere.

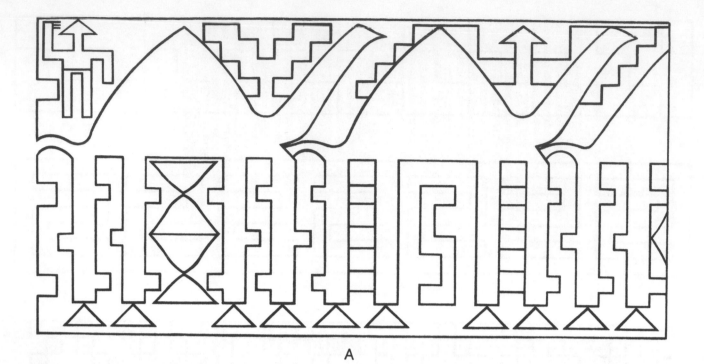

A

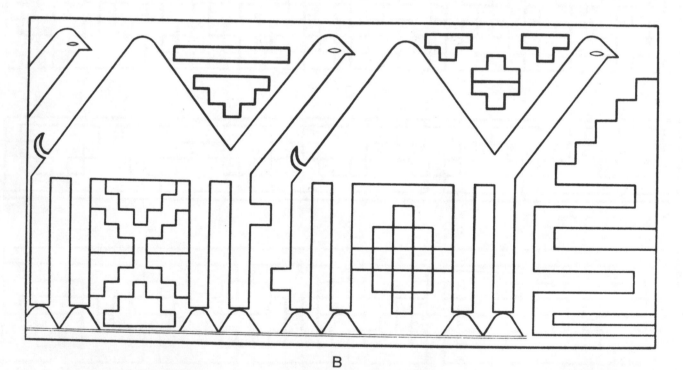

B

C

72   Gafsa textile motifs. A, B: Row of camels. C: Row of fish.

A

B

C

73 Gafsa patterns. From three *baṭṭānīya* blankets. A, B:
$133\frac{7}{8}'' \times 65\frac{3}{4}''$. C: $133\frac{1}{2}'' \times 71\frac{1}{8}''$.

74   Gafsa pattern. The two ends of a *ḥûli* blanket in the
Office des Arts Tunisiens, $205\frac{1}{2}'' \times 90\frac{7}{8}''$.

75 Gafsa pattern. The two ends of a *ḥûli* in the Office
des Arts Tunisiens, 196$\frac{7}{8}$″ × 85$\frac{1}{2}$″.

76   Gafsa pattern. The two ends of a *ḥûli* in the Office
des Arts Tunisiens, 133½″ × 67″.

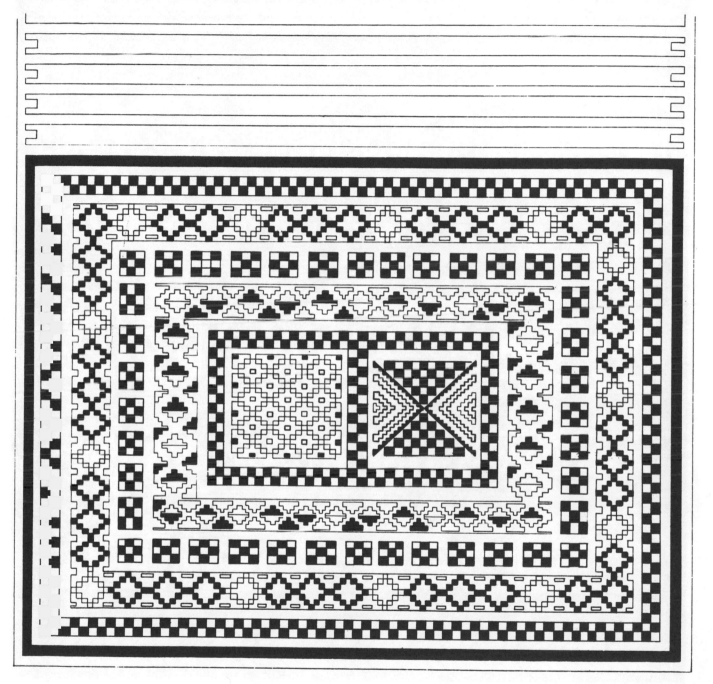

77 Gafsa pattern. One end of an antique *ḥûli* in the
Office des Arts Tunisiens, $84\frac{5}{8}'' \times 67''$.

78 Gafsa pattern. From a *ferrâšíya* blanket in the Office
des Arts Tunisiens, 90½″ × 88½″.

79 Gafsa pattern. From a *ferrāšíya* in the Office des
Arts Tunisiens, 102⅜″ × 86½″.

A

B

80   Gaſsa patterns. From *ferráſíya* blankets. A: 81½″ × 61″. B: 102⅜″ × 100⅜″.

81 Gafsa pattern. From a *ferrâšíya* in the Office des
Art Tunisiens, $91\frac{3}{8}'' \times 90\frac{1}{8}''$.

82   Gafsa pattern. From a *ferrâšíya* in the Office des
Arts Tunisiens, 89¾″ × 86½″.

83 Gafsa pattern. From a modern *ferrāšíya* in the Office
des Arts Tunisiens, 92½″ × 89¾″. Alternating white and
red backgrounds.

84   Gafsa pattern. From a *ferrâšíya* in the Office des
Arts Tunisiens, 92⅛″ × 87¼″.

85 Gafsa pattern. From a *ferrâšíya* in the Office des
Arts Tunisiens, 94½″ square.

86 Gafsa-type pattern from Sidi Bou Zid. From a modern *ḥûli* in the Office des Arts Tunisiens, 137¾″ × 65⅞″.

87 Kairouan flat-woven textile motifs. A: Brides, or rings. B: Sultan's banners. C: Sultan's banners with plumes. D: Plumed tortoises. E: Small flowered band. F: Spiders. G: Band with spiders and dots. H: Zigzag with triangles and feathers. I: Chick's eyes.

88 Kairouan flat-woven textile motifs. A: Adorned
brides. B: Couscous container. C: Band with feathers.
D: Band with carnations. E: Band with small banners.

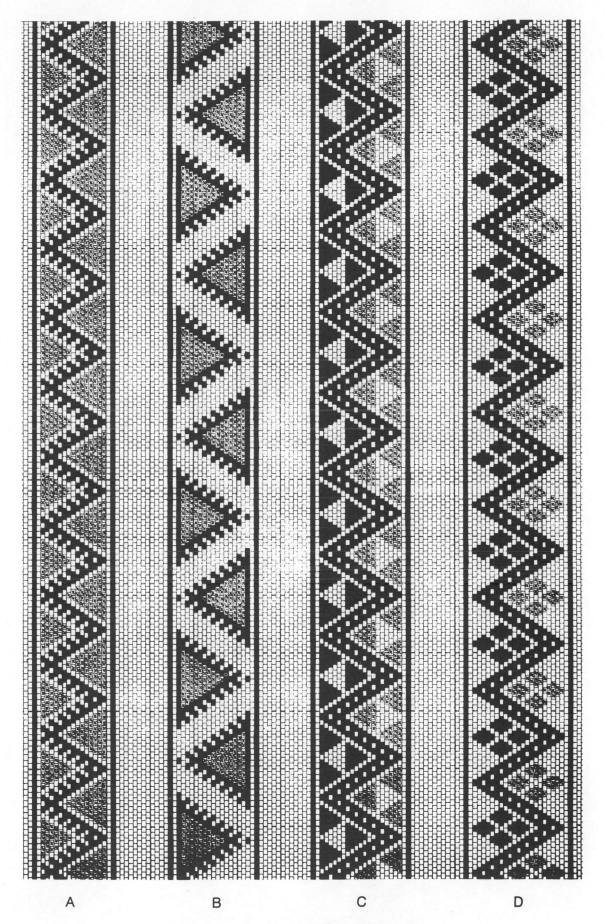

A   B   C   D

89 Kairouan flat-woven textile motifs. A: Sultan's
eyes. B: Amulets. C: Band of triangles. D: Apples.

A   B   C   D   E

90   Kairouan flat-woven textile motifs. A: Cat's footprints. B: Engraving on glass. C: Open hands. D: Fritters. E: Ribbed band.

A   B   C   D

91 Kairouan flat-woven textile motifs. A: Band with
dots. B: Couscous container with small dots. C: Tortoise
shells. D: Band with feathers.

A   B   C

92   Kairouan flat-woven textile motifs. A: Feather
band. B: Band with mother-of-pearl. C: Rings and
brides.

93   Kairouan flat-woven textile motifs. A: Small dots.
B: Tortoises.

94   Kairouan flat-woven textile motif: Banners.

95   Kairouan flat-woven textile motif: Plumed banners.

96   Kairouan flat-woven textile motif: Large plumed banners.

97   Kairouan flat-woven textile motif: Small dots.

A   B

98 Kairouan flat-woven textile motifs. A: Band of
non-interlocked triangles. B: Band of interlocked
triangles.

99 Kairouan flat-woven textile motif: Band with banners.

100 Kairouan flat-woven textile motif: Plumed band
with band of mother-of-pearl.

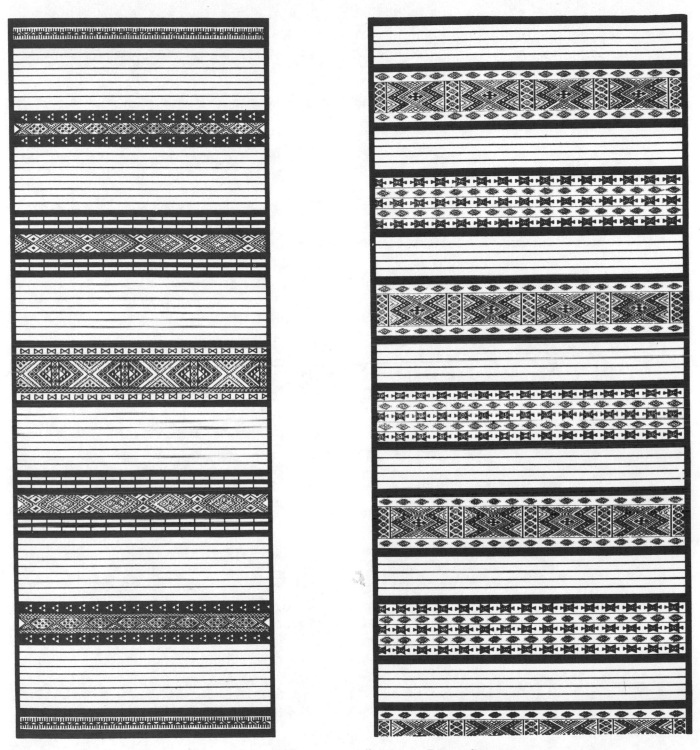

101 Kairouan flat-woven textile pattern. From a late
nineteenth-century *klim-mergûm* rug in Dar Ta^camallah,
Kairouan, 141¾″ × 51⅛″. Colors: red, black, violet,
yellow, green, orange, white.

102 Sâḥel flat-woven textile motifs. A, B: Beauty spots.
C: Scythe handle. D: Gazelle tracks. E: Foot tattoos. F:
Large fish bones. G–K: Fish bones.

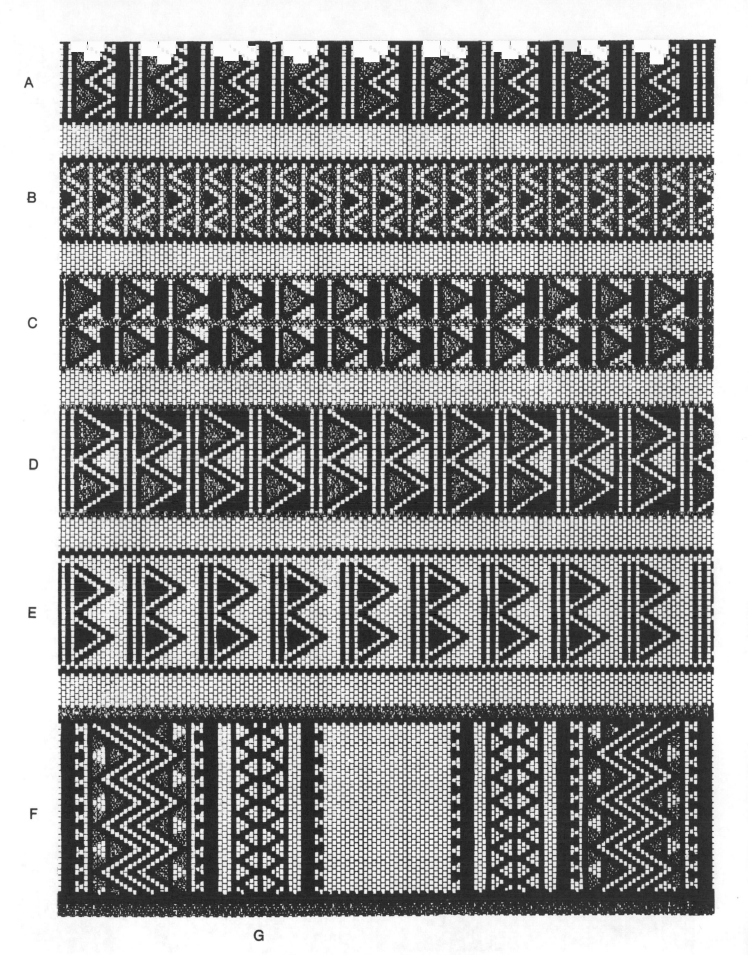

103 Sâhel flat-woven textile motifs. A, B, E: "Apprenticeship" motif. C: Sisters-in-law. D: Framed "apprenticeship" motif. F: Fish tails. G: "Occupation."

104 Sâḥel flat-woven textile motifs. A: Fish tails. B:
Multicolored kerchief. C: Framed "apprenticeship"
motif.

105 Sâḥel flat-woven textile motifs. A, B, D: Zigzags.
C: Carobs.

106 Sâḥel flat-woven textile motifs. A, D: Beans. B, C:
Simple amulets. E, F: Palm trees.

107 Sâhel flat-woven textile motifs. A, D: Clusters. B, C: Birds. E, F: Knucklebones. G, H: "Poor man's ankles." I: Boxes.

108 Sâḥel flat-woven textile motifs. A: Clusters with
eight points. B–E: Combs.

109.   Sâḥel flat-woven textile motifs. A: Clusters. B:
Small clusters. C: Clusters and "occupation." D: Clusters
with stone cubes.

110 Sâḥel flat-woven textile motifs: Three types of clusters.

111 Sâḥel flat-woven textile motifs. A: Clusters and "occupation." B–D: Clusters.

112 Sâḥel flat-woven textile motifs. A: "Moroccan clusters." B: Clusters.

113 Sâḥel flat-woven textile motifs. A: Brides. B: Bride.

114 Sâḥel flat-woven textile motifs. A: Flared motif.
B: Tattooing.

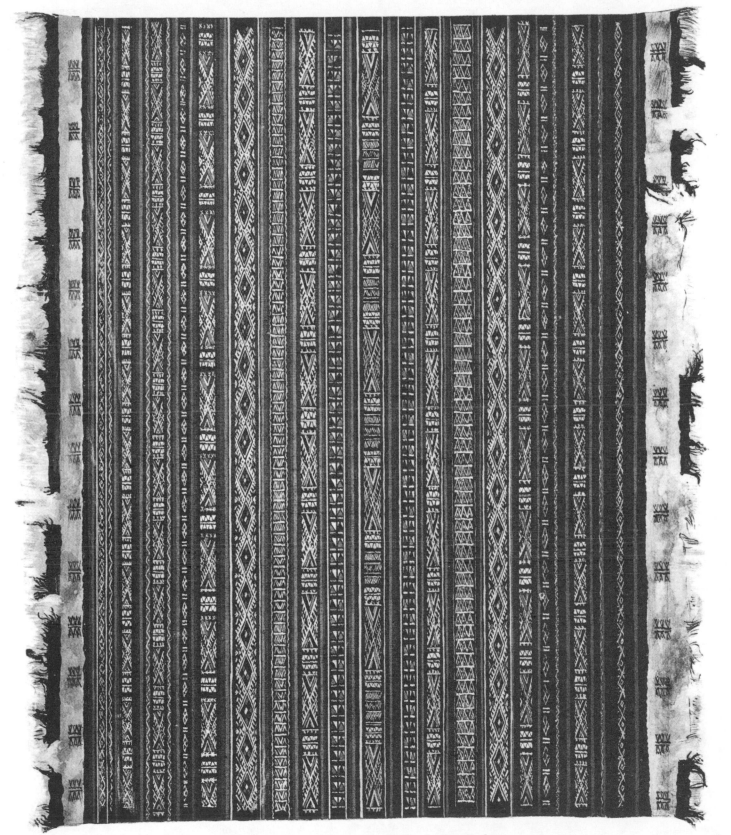

115 Late nineteenth-century *ûsâda* (cushion) from
El-Djem (in the Sâhel) in the Office des Arts Tunisiens,
Dar ʿOthman, 47¼″ × 35⅜″. Colors: red, orange, brown,
black, green, white.

116 Oudref flat-woven textile motifs. A: Groups of
houses, or small rings. B: Houses with scorpion stings, or
rings. C: "*Mergûm* design," or "*ḥambel* design" or
"bread design."

117   Oudref flat-woven textile motif: Stop, double decorated horn, scorpion with sorghum grains, edgings and
fish.

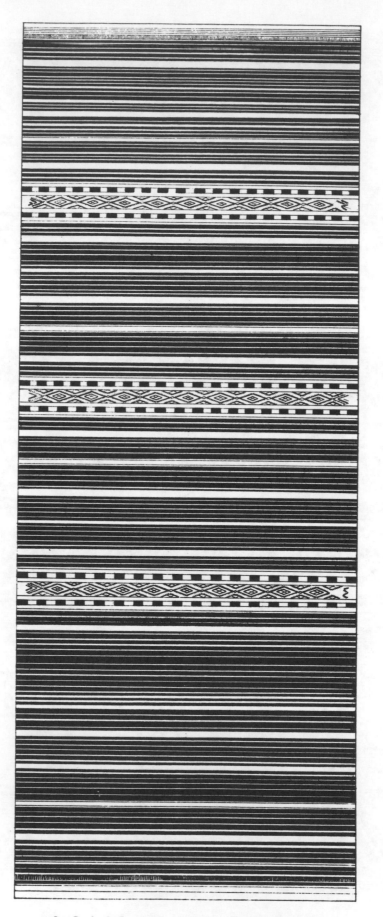

118 Oudref flat-woven pattern. From an antique
ḥambel blanket in the Office des Arts Tunisiens, Dar
ᶜOthman, 212⅝″ × 88⅝″. Colors: dark indigo blue,
black, madder red, green and white.

119 Oudref flat-woven pattern. From an antique *ûsâda* (cushion) in the Office des Arts Tunisiens, Dar ᶜOthman, $31\frac{1}{2}'' \times 20\frac{7}{8}''$. Colors: dark indigo blue and green, black, madder red and white.

120 Oudref flat-woven pattern. From a late nineteenth-century *klim* rug of the *jendâr* type in the Office des Arts Tunisiens, Centre de Gabès, 80¾″ × 44½″. The background is red; the designs and stripes are in black, blue, orange, yellow and white.

121 Motifs from local imitations in the Gafsa region of Oudref flat-woven textiles. A, B: "Ornament." C: "His hand in his brother's hand." D: Worms. E: Barred staircase. F: Couch.

Dover Books on Art

VITRUVIUS: TEN BOOKS ON ARCHITECTURE. The most influential book in the history of architecture. 1st century A.D. Roman classic has influenced such men as Bramante, Palladio, Michelangelo, up to present. Classic principles of design, harmony, etc. Fascinating reading. Definitive English translation by Professor H. Morgan, Harvard. 344pp. 5⅜ x 8.

20645-9 Paperbound $2.50

HAWTHORNE ON PAINTING. Vivid re-creation, from students' notes, of instructions by Charles Hawthorne at Cape Cod School of Art. Essays, epigrammatic comments on color, form, seeing, techniques, etc. "Excellent," Time. 100pp. 5⅜ x 8.

20653-X Paperbound $1.25

THE HANDBOOK OF PLANT AND FLORAL ORNAMENT, R. G. Hatton. 1200 line illustrations, from medieval, Renaissance herbals, of flowering or fruiting plants: garden flowers, wild flowers, medicinal plants, poisons, industrial plants, etc. A unique compilation that probably could not be matched in any library in the world. Formerly "The Craftsman's Plant-Book." Also full text on uses, history as ornament, etc. 548pp. 6⅛ x 9¼.

20649-1 Paperbound $4.50

DECORATIVE ALPHABETS AND INITIALS, Alexander Nesbitt. 91 complete alphabets, over 3900 ornamental initials, from Middle Ages, Renaissance printing, baroque, rococo, and modern sources. Individual items copyright free, for use in commercial art, crafts, design, packaging, etc. 123 full-page plates. 3924 initials. 129pp. 7¾ x 10¾.   20544-4 Paperbound $2.75

METHODS AND MATERIALS OF THE GREAT SCHOOLS AND MASTERS, Sir Charles Eastlake. (Formerly titled "Materials for a History of Oil Painting.") Vast, authentic reconstruction of secret techniques of the masters, recreated from ancient manuscripts, contemporary accounts, analysis of paintings, etc. Oils, fresco, tempera, varnishes, encaustics. Both Flemish and Italian schools, also British and French. One of great works for art historians, critics; inexhaustible mine of suggestions, information for practicing artists. Total of 1025pp. 5⅜ x 8.

20718-8, 20719-6 Two volume set, Paperbound $7.00

BYZANTINE ART AND ARCHAEOLOGY, O. M. Dalton. Still most thorough work in English on Byzantine art forms throughout ancient and medieval world. Analyzes hundreds of pieces, covers sculpture, painting, mosaic, jewelry, textiles, architecture, etc. Historical development; specific examples; iconology and ideas; symbolism. A treasure-trove of material about one of most important art traditions, will supplement and expand any other book in area. Bibliography of over 2500 items. 457 illustrations. 747pp. 6⅛ x 9¼.   20776-5 Clothbound $8.50

THE HUMAN FIGURE, J. H. Vanderpoel. Not just a picture book, but a complete course by a famous figure artist. Extensive text, illustrated by 430 pencil and charcoal drawings of both male and female anatomy. 2nd enlarged edition. Foreword. 430 illus. 143pp. 6⅛ x 9¼.   20432-4 Paperbound $1.50

GRAPHIC WORLDS OF PETER BRUEGEL THE ELDER,
H. A. Klein. 64 of the finest etchings and engravings made from
the drawings of the Flemish master Peter Bruegel. Every aspect
of the artist's diversified style and subject matter is represented,
with notes providing biographical and other background information. Excellent reproductions on opaque stock with nothing
on reverse side. 63 engravings, 1 woodcut. Bibliography. xviii +
289pp. 11⅜ x 8¼.   21132-0 Paperbound $4.00

THE COMPLETE WOODCUTS OF ALBRECHT DÜRER,
edited by Dr. Willi Kurth. Albrecht Dürer was a master in various media, but it was in woodcut design that his creative genius
reached its highest expression. Here are all of his extant woodcuts, a collection of over 300 great works, many of which are
not available elsewhere. An indispensable work for the art his-
torian and critic and all art lovers. 346 plates. Index. 285pp.
8½ x 12¼.   21097-9 Paperbound $4.00

GRAPHIC REPRODUCTION IN PRINTING, H. Curwen. A
behind-the-scenes account of the various processes of graphic
reproduction—relief, intaglio, stenciling, lithography, line
methods, continuous tone methods, photogravure, collotype—
and the advantages and limitations of each. Invaluable for all
artists, advertising art directors, commercial designers, adver-
tisers, publishers, and all art lovers who buy prints as a hobby.
137 illustrations, including 13 full-page plates, 10 in color. xvi +
171pp. 5¼ x 8½.   20512-6 Clothbound $7.50

WILD FOWL DECOYS, Joel Barber. Antique dealers, collectors,
craftsmen, hunters, readers of Americana, etc. will find this the
only thorough and reliable guide on the market today to this
unique folk art. It contains the history, cultural significance, re-
gional design variations; unusual decoy lore; working plans for
constructing decoys; and loads of illustrations. 140 full-page
plates, 4 in color. 14 additional plates of drawings and plans by
the author. xxvii + 156pp. 7⅞ x 10¾. 20011-6 Paperbound $4.00

1800 WOODCUTS BY THOMAS BEWICK AND HIS SCHOOL.
This is the largest collection of first-rate pictorial woodcuts in
print—an indispensable part of the working library of every
commercial artist, art director, production designer, packaging
artist, craftsman, manufacturer, librarian, art collector, and
artist. And best of all, when you buy your copy of Bewick, you
buy the rights to reproduce individual illustrations—no permis-
sion needed, no acknowledgments, no clearance fees! Classified
index. Bibliography and sources. xiv + 246pp. 9 x 12.

20766-8 Paperbound $4.00

THE SCRIPT LETTER, Tommy Thompson. Prepared by a noted
authority, this is a thorough, straightforward course of instruc-
tion with advice on virtually every facet of the art of script
lettering. Also a brief history of lettering with examples from
early copy books and illustrations from present day advertising
and packaging. Copiously illustrated. Bibliography. 128pp.
6½ x 9⅛.   21311-0 Paperbound $1.25

Dover Books on Art

PRINCIPLES OF ART HISTORY, H. Wölfflin. This remarkably instructive work demonstrates the tremendous change in artistic conception from the 14th to the 18th centuries, by analyzing 164 works by Botticelli, Dürer, Hobbema, Holbein, Hals, Titian, Rembrandt, Vermeer, etc., and pointing out exactly what is meant by "baroque," "classic," "primitive," "picturesque," and other basic terms of art history and criticism. "A remarkable lesson in the art of seeing," SAT. REV. OF LITERATURE. Translated from the 7th German edition. 150 illus. 254pp. 6⅛ x 9¼. 20276-3 Paperbound $2.50

FOUNDATIONS OF MODERN ART, A. Ozenfant. Stimulating discussion of human creativity from paleolithic cave painting to modern painting, architecture, decorative arts. Fully illustrated with works of Gris, Lipchitz, Léger, Picasso, primitive, modern artifacts, architecture, industrial art, much more. 226 illustrations. 368pp. 6⅛ x 9¼. 20215-1 Paperbound $3.00

METALWORK AND ENAMELLING, H. Maryon. Probably the best book ever written on the subject. Tells everything necessary for the home manufacture of jewelry, rings, ear pendants, bowls, etc. Covers materials, tools, soldering, filigree, setting stones, raising patterns, repoussé work, damascening, niello, cloisonné, polishing, assaying, casting, and dozens of other techniques. The best substitute for apprenticeship to a master metalworker. 363 photos and figures. 374pp. 5½ x 8½. 22702-2 Paperbound $3.50

SHAKER FURNITURE, E. D. and F. Andrews. The most illuminating study of Shaker furniture ever written. Covers chronology, craftsmanship, houses, shops, etc. Includes over 200 photographs of chairs, tables, clocks, beds, benches, etc. "Mr. & Mrs. Andrews know all there is to know about Shaker furniture," Mark Van Doren, NATION. 48 full-page plates. 192pp. 7⅞ x 10¾. 20679-3 Paperbound $2.75

LETTERING AND ALPHABETS, J. A. Cavanagh. An unabridged reissue of "Lettering," containing the full discussion, analysis, illustration of 89 basic hand lettering styles based on Caslon, Bodoni, Gothic, many other types. Hundreds of technical hints on construction, strokes, pens, brushes, etc. 89 alphabets, 72 lettered specimens, which may be reproduced permission-free. 121pp. 9¾ x 8. 20053-1 Paperbound $1.50

THE HUMAN FIGURE IN MOTION, Eadweard Muybridge. The largest collection in print of Muybridge's famous high-speed action photos. 4789 photographs in more than 500 action-strip-sequences (at shutter speeds up to 1/6000th of a second) illustrate men, women, children—mostly undraped—performing such actions as walking, running, getting up, lying down, carrying objects, throwing, etc. "An unparalleled dictionary of action for all artists," AMERICAN ARTIST. 390 full-page plates, with 4789 photographs. Heavy glossy stock, reinforced binding with headbands. 7⅞ x 10¾. 20204-6 Clothbound $12.50

Dover Books on Art

LANDSCAPE GARDENING IN JAPAN, Josiah Conder. A detailed picture of Japanese gardening techniques and ideas, the artistic principles incorporated in the Japanese garden, and the religious and ethical concepts at the heart of those principles. Preface. 92 illustrations, plus all 40 full-page plates from the Supplement. Index. xv + 299pp. 8⅜ x 11¼.

21216-5   Paperbound $3.50

DESIGN AND FIGURE CARVING, E. J. Tangerman. "Anyone who can peel a potato can carve," states the author, and in this unusual book he shows you how, covering every stage in detail from very simple exercises working up to museum-quality pieces. Terrific aid for hobbyists, arts and crafts counselors, teachers, those who wish to make reproductions for the commercial market. Appendix: How to Enlarge a Design. Brief bibliography. Index. 1298 figures. x + 289pp. 5⅜ x 8½.

21209-2   Paperbound $2.00

THE STANDARD BOOK OF QUILT MAKING AND COLLECTING, M. Ickis. Even if you are a beginner, you will soon find yourself quilting like an expert, by following these clearly drawn patterns, photographs, and step-by-step instructions. Learn how to plan the quilt, to select the pattern to harmonize with the design and color of the room, to choose materials. Over 40 full-size patterns. Index. 483 illustrations. One color plate. xi + 276pp. 6¾ x 9½.   20582-7   Paperbound $2.50

LOST EXAMPLES OF COLONIAL ARCHITECTURE, J. M. Howells. This book offers a unique guided tour through America's architectural past, all of which is either no longer in existence or so changed that its original beauty has been destroyed. More than 275 clear photos of old churches, dwelling houses, public buildings, business structures, etc. 245 plates, containing 281 photos and 9 drawings, floorplans, etc. New Index. xvii + 248pp. 7⅞ x 10¾.   21143-6   Paperbound $3.00

A HISTORY OF COSTUME, Carl Köhler. The most reliable and authentic account of the development of dress from ancient times through the 19th century. Based on actual pieces of clothing that have survived, using paintings, statues and other reproductions only where originals no longer exist. Hundreds of illustrations, including detailed patterns for many articles. Highly useful for theatre and movie directors, fashion designers, illustrators, teachers. Edited and augmented by Emma von Sichart. Translated by Alexander K. Dallas. 594 illustrations. 464pp. 5⅛ x 7⅛.

21030-8   Paperbound $3.00

Dover publishes books on commercial art, art history, crafts, design, art classics; also books on music, literature, science, mathematics, puzzles and entertainments, chess, engineering, biology, philosophy, psychology, languages, history, and other fields. For free circulars write to Dept. DA, Dover Publications, Inc., 180 Varick St., New York, N.Y. 10014.

175650

...orth African carpets & textiles.
New York, Dover Publications [1973]
    xii p., 121 p. of illus. 29 cm. (Dover pictorial archive series)
$3.50
    "New selection ... of plates from the four portfolios of Tapis
tunisiens, by L. Poinssot and J. Revault."
    1. Design, Decorative—Tunisia. 2. Rugs, Tunisian. 3. Textile
industry and fabrics, Tunisian.   I. Poinssot, Louis. Tapis tunisiens. II. Title.
NK1487.85.A1R48   1973   746.7'961'1   72–93604
ISBN 0–486–22850–9   R32   MARC